LIVEWIRE
REAL LIVES

Michael Owen

Andy Croft

Published in association with The Basic Skills Agency

Hodder & Stoughton

A MEMBER OF THE HODDER HEADLINE GROUP

Acknowledgements

Cover: © Ellis O'Brien/All Action

Photos: pp 2, 10, 13, 27 Paul McFegan/Allstar; p7 Monte Fresco/Popperfoto; p18 Stewart Kendall/Allstar;,p 20 Joiner/Popperfoto; p 23 Popperfoto

Every effort has been made to trace copyright holders of material reproduced in this book. Any rights not acknowledged will be acknowledged in subsequent printings if notice is given to the publisher.

Orders; please contact Bookpoint Ltd, 39 Milton Park, Abingdon, Oxon OX14 4TD. Telephone: (44) 01235 400414, Fax: (44) 01235 400454. Lines are open from 9.00–6.00, Monday to Saturday, with a 24 hour message answering service. Email address: orders@bookpoint.co.uk

British Library Cataloguing in Publication Data
A catalogue record for this title is available from the British Library

ISBN 0 340 77661 7

First published 2000
Impression number   10 9 8 7 6 5 4 3 2 1
Year   2005 2004 2003 2002 2001 2000

Copyright © 2000 Andy Croft

Typeset by GreenGate Publishing Services, Tonbridge, Kent.
Printed in Great Britain for Hodder and Stoughton Educational, a division of Hodder Headline Plc, 338 Euston Road, London NW1 3BH, by Redwood Books, Trowbridge, Wilts

Contents

1 Birth of a Legend

Michael James Owen
was born on 14 December 1979
in the village of Hawarden near Chester.

His Dad Terry used to play football
for Everton, Bradford, Chester, Rochdale
and Port Vale.

Michael supported Everton as a boy.
His hero was Everton
and England striker Gary Lineker.

Michael wanted to play for
Everton and England like Gary Lineker.
He hoped that one day he would be
as good as Gary Lineker.

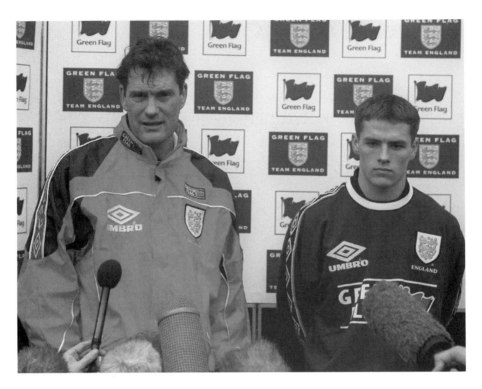

Glen Hoddle picked Michael for his England squad.

1 Record Breaker

Michael Owen started playing football
when he was six.

He was small,
but he was brilliant.
He used both feet.
He was fast and brave.
He could turn defenders.
He could shoot from anywhere.

He was picked for his school team
when he was in Y3.

He started playing for
Mold Alexandra under-10s
when he was only seven.
He came on as a sub in his first game,
and he scored.
He scored 34 goals in 28 games for Mold.
He scored 9 goals in one game.
The manager once put him in goal,
just to be kind to the other team!

His Dad took him to a boxing club
to make him tougher.
He only had two fights.
He won them both,
but his nose was broken.

He played for
Deesside Primary Schools under-11s
when he was only eight.
He scored 72 goals in one season.
This beat the Deesside record
held by Liverpool's Ian Rush.

He played a record number of games
for them in one season.
This beat the record held
by Newcastle's Gary Speed.

3 Excellence

Lots of clubs wanted to sign him,
especially Man United and Arsenal
but he chose Liverpool.
They asked him to train at their
Centre of Excellence.
He was still only ten.
Liverpool legend Steve Highway
was the coach.

At the age of 14 Michael joined
the FA School of Excellence
at Lilleshall.

He was picked to play for the
England under-15 and under-16 teams.
He scored 12 goals in one season
for the under-16s.
Another record.

'Caps Day' at Lilleshall. Michael is presented with his
England cap by Dario Gradi.

He played for the England under-18 team
when he was only 16.
He scored all four goals in his first match.

Michael Owen worked hard at school.
He passed 10 GCSEs.
He could have taken A Levels.
He could have gone to university.
But when he was 16
he signed for Liverpool.
They only paid him £42 a week.

He only played five games for the
Liverpool Youth team
but he scored 11 goals.
That season, Liverpool won the FA Youth Cup.

Michael signed for Liverpool
on his 17th birthday.

4 Liverpool

A few months later
he made his debut for Liverpool
against Wimbledon at Selhurst Park.
He started on the bench
and came on in the second half.
Twenty minutes later he ran clear
of the Wimbledon defence.
He turned and shot –
GOAL!
He was the youngest goal scorer
in the club's history.

He scored again on the opening day
of the next season against Wimbledon.

A few weeks later he made his European debut
against Celtic in the UEFA Cup.
After six minutes he ran onto a pass from Riedle.
He beat the defence
and lifted the ball over the keeper.
GOAL!

Ince and Owen

He scored his first hat-trick
against Grimsby in the League Cup.
He scored his first League hat-trick
against Sheffield Wednesday.

That season he was joint top scorer
in the Premiership
with 23 League and Cup goals.

He was voted Young Player of the Year
and Player of the Year.

Because he is small, some people
called him 'the Midget Gem'!

5 England Expects

Michael had already played
for the England under-15s, under-16s,
under-18s and under-21s teams.

On 11 February 1998
he made his full debut for England
in a friendly against Chile.
He was only 18 years and 59 days old.
He was the youngest England player
this century.
He almost scored
but England lost the game 2–0.

Michael made his debut for England.

He played more friendlies,
against Switzerland and Belgium.
He came on as a sub against Portugal.
His pace scared the Portuguese defenders.
He was tripped
but the ref did not give a penalty.

He came on as a sub against Morocco.
This time he scored.
It was his first goal for England.
It wasn't his last.

6 World Cup

The World Cup was held in France in 1998.
Glen Hoddle picked Michael for his squad.
England fans wanted Michael to start,
but Hoddle kept him on the bench.
Michael Owen was his secret weapon.

He came on against Tunisia
with six minutes to go
and helped England win 2–0.

He came on against Romania
in the 73rd minute.
Ten minutes later he ran onto the ball.
He turned and shot,
GOAL!

He started against Colombia
and helped England win 2–0.

England and Michael Owen were through
to the second round of the World Cup.

7 Goal!

England had to play Argentina
in the next round.
The match was played
on a hot night in June.
The crowd was excited.
So was the press.
But Michael Owen was calm.
He knew what he had to do.

After only six minutes
Argentina were given a penalty.
Batistuta scored.
Four minutes later Michael was brought down
in the Argentine box.
Alan Shearer scored from the spot.

Alan Shearer and Owen

Six minutes later he ran onto a pass
from David Beckham.
He ran 50 yards through the Argentine defence.
He held off Chamot,
he went round Ayala,
he shot past Carlos Roa.
GOAL!
It was the best goal of the World Cup.
It was the goal of a life-time.

Michael holds off Chamot of Argentina on the run that led to him scoring the second goal.

In the second half Argentina equalised.
After extra time it went to penalties.
Michael took the fourth England penalty.
It went in off the post.
GOAL!

Argentina won 4–3 on penalties.
England were out.
But no-one will ever forget
Michael Owen's goal.

8 Anfield

Michael Owen was now very famous.
People said he was 'the new Ronaldo'.
Juventus and Real Madrid wanted to buy him
but he only wanted to play for Liverpool.
He only wanted to play at Anfield.

After all, he had only played one season
for the club.
He loves the Reds.

The next season he scored a hat-trick
against Newcastle.
He scored four goals against Notts Forest.
He scored 21 goals in 39 games.

1998 World Cup Finals. Michael beats Tunisia's Mounir
Boukadida.

Liverpool had some brilliant players:
James, Redknapp, Fowler, MacManaman,
Ince, Matteo, Berger, Riedle, Owen.

But they couldn't win anything.
Not even with Michael Owen.

Liverpool have a new manager.
His name is Gerard Houlier.
He has begun to rebuild the team.
He has bought some players.
He has sold some players
but Michael Owen is not for sale.

Can Michael Owen help to make
Liverpool great again?

9 The Future

Michael Owen is one of the richest young players
in British football.
He earns £20,000 a week.
That's a million pounds a year.

He advertises watches and sportswear.
Fans send him hundreds of letters every week.
He has a computer game named after him.
He has presented his own TV series.
His World Cup shirt was sold for £2,000.
His legs are so valuable
that Liverpool can't insure them!

He still lives near his Mum and Dad
in Chester.
He is still going out with Louise.
They started going out when they were at school.

Michael likes eating pasta and chinese food.
He has a dog called Bomber.
He likes listening to the Lightening Seeds.
His favourite film is *Cool Runnings*.
His favourite actors are
Eddie Murphy and Rik Mayall.
He likes playing snooker,
table-tennis and golf.
He can beat all the other England players
at golf.

Michael Owen is an ordinary young man,
but he has extraordinary talent.
He may be small,
but he has big ambitions.

Not just for himself,
but for Liverpool
and for England.